LONDON
AT DAWN

Anthony Epes

LONDON AT DAWN

Anthony Epes

Published by Metro Publishing Ltd,
3 Bramber Court, 2 Bramber Road,
London W14 9PB, England

First published in hardback in 2002

ISBN 1 84358 036 5

British Library Cataloguing-in-Publication Data:
A catalogue record for this book is available
from the British Library.

Design by ENVY

Printed and bound in Italy by Eurolitho S.p.A

1 3 5 7 9 10 8 6 4 2

www.anthonyepes.com

Papers used by Metro Publishing Ltd are natural,
recyclable products made from wood grown in sustainable forests.
The manufacturing processes conform to the environmental
regulations of the country of origin.

Every attempt has been made to contact the relevant
copyright-holders, but some were unobtainable. We would
be grateful if the appropriate people could contact us.

ACKNOWLEDGEMENTS

The early hours of the morning embrace a serenity, regardless of what lies ahead in the day, be it sunshine and wind, clouds and rain or the bustling of people on their way.

London is a city of great beauty, both obvious and at the same time elusive. Many of the places I travelled to for this book are places seen countless times by innumerable people but rarely seen in the dawn hours. My ambition is to share with you the thrill to stand and observe the beauty that costs nothing and gives much. If you look at images in this book and feel a desire for that time and place then I have succeeded.

The *London At Dawn* project is the culmination of much dedication and hard work, not all my own. I would like to take this time to thank all those involved. John and Grant at Metro Soho, Daniel Rubenstein at Photofusion for his expertise and advice, Phil Bingham for his friendship and research, Anita Mangan for her opinion and support, Tessa Swithinbank for her tireless efforts in collecting and compiling the texts, Barney Allan for his guidance and getting the deal, Tony Cook and all the staff at Burgeon Creative, Sarah Brown for organising and the follow-ups. Special thanks to: John Blake for believing in the project and taking it on, Nick Mortimer for the friendship, support and picking me up at 2am – cheers mate! John Bird for the opportunity and the idea.

I would like to thank my family – Mary, Jack, Litha, Barney and Aidan – for all the love and patience the world has to offer. Lastly, my wife Diana, I thank for everything you do.

Anthony Epes

FOREWORD

I am a dawn man. I am either there because I have been up all night, or because I have some early morning tasks.

I have always been involved in early morning London. As a coal deliverer in suburban Fulham, as a butcher boy, taking meat to the big houses of Knightsbridge or buying meat for restaurants at Smithfields. I have also slept in the streets and haunted the cafés and bars of Covent Garden. I have walked aimlessly from one all-night café to another. Or from station waiting rooms to street coffee stalls.

Anthony Epes's photographs capture, for me, very fine feelings that are London at dawn. Its dignity. Its abundant, though at times hidden, nature. Its great beauty, and the depth of its history. There is something magical about London at dawn, and Anthony's photographs expose some of that magic. If you look carefully at these pictures, you will see that beauty. That arriving, hopeful, exciting day. The pulse of London exists just beyond these photographs. Anthony's photographs capture that anticipation.

My favourite among this collection is from the door of St Paul's. Its blueness is almost exotic. Its sense of being is thoughtful. It hesitates before the arrival of traffic and people. It is magnificent.

And London, that magnificent city, has found a great interpreter: Anthony Epes.

A John Bird

Thames Flood Barrier

When will the
dead world
cease to dream,
When will the
morning break?

WILLIAM WINTER, 'THE NIGHT WATCH'

Boat on Thames
by Flood Barrier

It was between six and seven in the morning. The moon was low in the sky. It was a waxing moon, a gibbous one; it was a particular moon. I raised the window-blind. The pinky-orange hibiscus street lamp outside the window was the same as always. I opened the front door and went out into the foredawn, into the hissing of the silence and the humming of the Underground trains, standing empty with lighted windows, on the far side of the common. Unseen birds twittered but there was no crow to shout and flaunt its blackness.

I heard my footsteps; I saw under the lamps my shadow, first before me, then behind. 'Nothing to declare,' I said.

I crossed the common and headed down the New King's Road. The Belisha beacons slicked as they blinked in the coldness of the morning. Cars at intervals hissed past me, in each one a face as questionable as the faces printed on the tiny windows of toy cars from Japan. The shops stood like sleeping horses.

The lamps on Putney Bridge were still lit, the bridge stood in simple astonishment over the water, a stonelike creature of overness, of parapets and ghostly-pale, cool tones of blue, of grey, of dim whiteness in the foredawn, with its lamps lit against a sky growing light. Far below lay the river; slack-water it was, turn of the tide, the low-tide river narrow between expanses of mud, the moored boats rocking on the stillness.

A sort of singing filled my head; it seemed an aspect of the particles of light and colour that made in my eyes the picture of this time just before dawn. I thought of the dew on the grass where the olive tree stood. There seemed to be a question in the air.

'Yes,' I said, 'I will.' I spoke aloud because I wanted my answer to be recorded on the early air.

I was walking on the Putney side of the river, walking on the low-tide beach, hearing the lapping of the water on the stones. I was seeing the moon-glints on the water, I was smelling the low-tide smell of the mud and the stones by the river.

The singing in my head became the slowly spreading circles of an intolerable clangour; it was as if the brute bell of the universe were caged in my mind and bursting my skull. 'Eurydice!' whispered a voice from the mud, from the stones. 'Eurydice!'

RUSSELL HOBAN, 'FINDING THE HEAD OF ORPHEUS NEAR PUTNEY BRIDGE AT DAWN', FROM *THE MEDUSA FREQUENCY*

Give me the splendid silent sun, with all his beams full-dazzling!

WALT WHITMAN,
'GIVE ME THE SPLENDID SILENT SUN'

Relic on the Thames

Moss and Ropes

Drain and Rope

Shopping carts on Thames banks

Thank you
for asking me,
but I don't
like London.
It sucks.

JULIE BURCHILL

Take thy thoughts to bed with thee, for the morning is wiser than the evening.

RUSSIAN PROVERB

Homes in Docklands

Each morning sees some task begin,
Each evening sees it close
Something attempted, something done,
Has earned a night's repose.

FROM 'THE VILLAGE BLACKSMITH'
HENRY WADSWORTH LONGFELLOW

Blackheath Tea-hut

Naval Museum, Greenwich

Tyres on Thames banks

Thames wash – suds of heaven,
swirled,
washing pebbles, mixing tarry shores.
No ugly death disfigurement. The oily damp like
sweat in slickness,
clinging dark
green moss to slimy stones.

A single tyre crouched midst this hungry land,
Entombed in silt in sifting sand and
waiting.
Rolling into darkness in my dreams,
to vacant ground – the memory of salt,
the sea-like tide, that dips and wells
round polystyrene cups and shells.
We treasure hunt as daybreak cloaks,
As sunlight soaks, the haunted verse,
the shaken hour, the time
that's left.
Bereft the shoreline,
Parched yet drenched.
Remote yet close, so tightly held
when sadness swiftly runs
in mists, and fogs who gathered
tears in vale, abandon remnants.
Sky so pale,
Remember, this –
the daybreak view,
these words though few,
encompass.

JUDE EYDMANN,
'THAMES BANKS' SUNRISE'

Cranes at Canary Wharf

There is a reassurance in the dawn.

There is something truly wonderful about going to work in the dark and coming home in daylight. It's as if the world has been tilted away from normal and everything is ever so slightly but specially different.

We looked forward to the dawn in the Accident and Emergency Department. We looked forward to the chance to rest for a moment without the electric charge of the cardiac arrest alarm or an ambulance coming in on the twotones. Either sound would make us leap to our feet like the best of Pavlov's dogs and we would rush for the CA trolley or the doors to the ambulance bay. It was never good news and we did the job on adrenaline and routine.

Every night had its own rhythm between 10 and 6am. Blood and bodies on the decks when the pubs emptied out, the lost the lonely and the broken drifting into the only open door in W1 when the shutters had gone up and the bouncers were out in the West End.

The suicide hour after 3am when the still, dark night of the soul is too much to endure and the dying hour between four and five when people seemed to simply slip their moorings and drift out to meet death before the daylight comes. The shrieking and the shouting was always loudest in the darkest part of the night, and our priority was patching them and protecting ourselves for most of the shift. From the sky it must have looked like a floodlit anthill surrounded by silence and darkness. Inside it was often carnage, sometimes boring, but always real. A place of life and of death.

As the night wore on the furious friends of the pub fighters drifted away, and we started to see the quiet confused, who'd had a call to come down quickly, but were often just too late. They had a different life ahead of them. We had the morning to look forward to.

The early shift would come on a few minutes early for changeover and we'd go through the horrors of the night and tell the human tales that are always lost in the official record. Then we'd change out of the stained and bloody uniforms, queue at the time clock and walk slowly into the searchlight of the sun. While the rest of the world was going to work we went our separate ways, by bus and bike and tube. Two of us always walked down through Soho to Covent Garden tube. It wasn't the nearest but we liked it.

We liked to see the bread on the restaurant doorsteps, and the milk and vegetables being delivered. Best of all, we saw the streets coming alive after the brief hibernation of the night to a background sound of ever louder traffic and the smell of new brewed coffee.

When you spend your night with death you need to know that life can be as strong, and when you try to mend the broken hearts and bodies you need to see the other side. To see the beating heart of London in the dawn was our antidote to the pain from those other hearts that had stopped beyond resuscitation not so long ago.

However terrible things had been, and would be again, the day would dawn, the sun would rise and the city would stretch and wake to face another day. Maybe all cities are the same, but London is my home and I felt, and still feel, part of that one body. London can be cruel and unforgiving, but she gives us a fresh, clean start every morning and however harshly the city treats us I will always love her.

STEVE POUND, MP FOR EALING NORTH (FROM 1997),
WHO WORKED AT UNIVERSITY COLLEGE HOSPITAL AND
THE MIDDLESEX HOSPITAL FROM 1971 TO 1979

Come,
lovely morning,
Rich in frost,
on iron,
wood and glass ...

W.H. DAVIES,
'SILVER HOURS'

Buildings in Fog at Canary Wharf

At daybreak Morn shall come to me In raiment of the white winds spun.

Quiet

MADISON JULIUS CAWEIN

Cranes in Fog at Canary Wharf

Two black owls
came and perched
on battlements,
remained there
through night
hooting, at dawn
flew away ...

MAX BEERBOHM,
'ZULEIKA DOBSON'

Building in Moon and Fog

What time finds me now?

This golden show is not anew that draws shallow shadows in my name.

This light had never gone, we had turned away.

What time of the city is this?

The sound is nothing new. The beat of feet on streets is still the same

The life has never gone, it changes with the day.

My time in the city is gone

I never had to move this fast to find a space

To chase my precious moments where they led.

Converse with air in hurried tones at pace

And count, again, the thirty bits of silver in my head.

I never pressed a button save to dress

Or surfed a world that sat inside a box

You spend your moments trying to impress

Your mark upon a city run by clocks.

I've been in this city so long

Watched raindrops wear this very stone away and, so, we all must take a turn

To feel the days pass on before we know.

So life in the city is you?

Who claims the world was leading to today, for you, and yet you never learn

This city stays, it's you who come and go.

ELY WHITLEY, 'CAMDEN CEMETERY'

Camberwell Cemetery

Camberwell Cemetery

I hate the day,
because it
lendeth light
To see all things,
but not my
love to see.

EDMUND SPENSER,
FROM 'DAPHNAIDA'

I hear beyond
the range of sound,
I see beyond the
range of sight,
New earths
and skies and
seas around,
And in my day the
sun doth pale
his light.

HENRY DAVID THOREAU

View in East Dulwich

There's a little piece of London where I regularly watch the dawn come up. A patch of land, longer than it's wide, it's the back garden of the terraced house in Islington where I live with my partner, theatre director Greg Doran.

I'm a bad sleeper. Especially when I'm writing a book; an experience that's not unlike a drug, fever or infatuation – you become totally possessed. So I often find myself rising early to continue grappling with some latest fixation. The work is accompanied by two factors which intensify the buzz: far too many cups of coffee, and the spectacle of a London dawn. I view this through the glass roof of my basement study, which pushes into the garden like a sunken conservatory. In summer it's already fully light by 5am; that remarkably low, still sunshine which, framed by a tangle of roses or ivy, rests on the old bricks of the garden wall with the glow of an antique photograph, inviting you to think about all the other people who might have stared at that spot in former times. Our terrace was built as artisans' dwellings in 1824, so this house must have held many generations of dawn-watchers: some getting up to work, some revelling through the night, some making love, some dying, some being born. In winter it's still pitch black out there at five, and will remain so for hours to come; a dense, cold, northern-hemisphere black which alarms my African sensibilities (I was born in Cape Town) as much as the early summer sun enchants them. In Africa dawns and dusks are fast affairs. The world springs in and out of focus in a strikingly dramatic way. Here in England the sun behaves like the people do, with more subtlety and repose.

If the weather's warm enough, I'll go out into the garden to write, or to learn lines when I'm preparing for a role. Not wanting to disturb the neighbours, I speak in a whisper. Pacing round and round in my dressing gown, incessantly muttering Shakespeare or Stoppard, Marlowe or Mike Leigh, I feel like some kind of wizard or sangoma, invoking the spirits, casting a spell. Our garden does have a rather magical aspect – it's almost like a secret garden – being open and sunny near the house, then seeming to narrow more than perspective demands, over the patio and lawn, past the tall dog-rose to one side, the cherry tree to the other, curling and closing into a leafy dark hollow at the far end.

I cherish it. Although I have no gardening skills whatsoever (a young American lady called Brooke tends it for us), I love owning a tiny piece of earth, of ground, of nature, in this big metropolitan city. The garden is where I can still see and hear the real world. Squirrels nest in the big sycamore trees that separate our property from those in the next street, and fearless little robins hop onto the wrought-iron table where I work. Seagulls sometimes fly over – my Cape Town spirit lifting to their cry – and one autumn a tremendous flock of Canada geese went by, almost blanking out the light. On another occasion a giant heron – perhaps an escapee from Regent's Park zoo – suddenly landed on the neighbour's wall to survey their fish pond, and perched there for a while, looking so incongruous and out-of-scale it could have been from prehistoric times.

As I write this piece now, down in the study, it's a grim February day, and London lies beneath one of those blank grey skies which were perfectly described by Bill Bryson when he said that the British live under tupperware. At this time of year, I yearn for African light and heat, yearn till I hurt, but I think it's just a question of still having to learn another quintessentially English

quality: patience. A day will come when I'll be sitting down here before dawn, and I'll glance up from my computer and notice that the northern blackness is giving way to faint golds, pinks and blues. I'll unlock the back door, and there'll be something in the air ... a kind of scent, a kind of breeze ... an unmistakable change. When spring arrives, this garden, and the whole city, will become one of the loveliest places imaginable. In Africa, sunshine is commonplace. Here it's a rare thing, carrying with it a sense of privilege, of blessing. In springtime I'm always very happy being a Londoner again.

SIR ANTONY SHER

Dulwich Village

The parks are the lungs of London.

WILLIAM PITT
THE YOUNGER

Grass and Leaves

Swan in the East

All the
birds will sing
at dawn.

ELIZABETH BARRETT BROWNING,
'AURORA LEIGH'

It's the birds
that make London
at dawn. I love the
pigeons and
sparrows. I love the
crows. Walking in
the early morning,
seeing and hearing
the birds – that's
London at dawn.

SARAH LUCAS

The piece of London which I hold in my heart is a part I have never lived in – Whitechapel. But it's the real East End, where my Jewish great-grandfather came to live, in Goodmans Fields, in the 1860s. So much of the Jewish culture I absorbed came from this area – small shopkeepers, kosher chickens on a slab, salt beef sandwiches from the now-closed Blooms Restaurant, little synagogues in small streets like Princelet St – and lively street markets with witty stall holders shouting their wares with flair and cunning. The dirty blocks of apartment buildings, all stairs and washing lines, Brick Lane, Leman St, Black Lion Yard – these are the streets of my family history. And now, another people have taken over – with their food, their stories – from places further away than Posen and Berlin. I grew up in Oxford – quite another feel to that place – but the emotional heart of London for me is the gritty, warm-hearted East End.

MIRIAM MARGOLYES

View from Shoreditch Station off Brick Lane

Lorry on Brick Lane

Butlers Wharf

'Yes,' I answered
you last night;
'No,' this morning,
sir, I say:
Colours seen by
candle-light
Will not look the
same by day.

ELIZABETH BARRETT BROWNING,
'THE LADY'S YES'

Butlers Wharf

When did
morning
ever break,
And find such
beaming eyes
awake?

THOMAS MOORE,
'FLY NOT YET'

Syd's Coffee Stand in Hackney

I like the lad, who when
his father thought
To clip his morning nap
by hackneyed phrase
Of vagrant worm by
early songster caught
Cried, 'Served him right!
It's not at all surprising
The worm was punished,
Sir, for early rising!'

JOHN GODFREY SAXE,
'EARLY RISING'

Entrance to Lloyds Building

It is true,
I never assisted
the sun materially
in his rising;
but, doubt not, it
was of the last
importance only to
be present at it.

HENRY DAVID THOREAU

Window washer at Lloyds

There are painters
who transform the sun
into a yellow spot,
but there are others who,
thanks to their art and
intelligence, transform a
yellow spot into the sun.

PABLO PICASSO

Tower Bridge from Sugar Quay

Tower Bridge from HMS *Belfast*

I saw two clouds at morning,
Tinged with the rising sun,
And in the dawn they floated on,
And mingled into one.
I thought that morning cloud was blest,
It moved so sweetly to the West.

JOHN GARDINER CALKINS BRAINARD,
'EPITHALAMIUM'

Our lives are like
the course of the sun.
At the darkest moment
there is the promise
of daylight.

LONDON *TIMES*
(CHRISTMAS EDITORIAL)

Tunnel by London Bridge

London Bridge Station

In the morning, when thou art sluggish at rousing thee, let this thought be present; 'I am rising to a man's work.'

MARCUS AURELIUS,
FROM 'MEDITATIONS'

Coming up in London Bridge Station

Bank of England

London, thou art of townes A per se.
Soveraign of cities, semeliest in sight,
Of high renoun, riches and royaltie;
Of lordis, barons, and many a goodly knyght;
Of most delectable lusty ladies bright;
Of famous prelatis, in habitis clericall;
Of merchauntis full of substaunce and myght:
London, thou art the Flour of Cities all.

Gladdith anon, thou lusty Troynovaunt,
Citie that some tyme cleped was New Troy,
In all the erth, imperiall as thou stant,
Pryncesse of townes, of pleasure and of joy,
A richer restith under no Christen roy;
For manly power, with craftis naturall,
Fourmeth none fairer sith the flode of Noy:
London, thou art the Flour of Cities all.

Gemme of all joy, jasper of jocunditie,
Most myghty carbuncle of vertue and valour,
Strong Troy in vigour and in strenuytie;
Of royall cities rose and geraflour;
Empresse of townes, exalt in honour,
In beautie berying the crone imperiall;
Swete paradise precelling in pleasure;
London, thou art the Flour of Cities all.

Above all ryuers thy Ryuer hath renowne,
Whose beryall stremys, pleasant and preclare,
Under thy lusty wallys renneth down,
Where many a swanne doth swymme with wyngis fair;
Where many a barge doth saile and row with are,
Where many a ship doth rest with toppe-royall.
O! towne of townes, patrone and not compare:
London, thou art the Flour of Cities all.

Upon thy lusty Brigge of pylers white
Been merchauntis full royall to behold;
Upon thy stretis goeth many a semely knyght
(Arrayit) in velvet gownes and in cheynes of gold.
By Julyus Cesar thy Tour founded of old
May be the Hous of Mars victoryall,
Whos artillary with tonge may not be told:
London, thou art the Flour of Cities all.

Strong be thy wallys that about thee standis;
Wise be the people that within thee dwellis;
Fresh is they ryuer with his lusty strandis;
Blith be thy churches, wele sownyng be thy bellis;
Rich be thy merchauntis in substaunce that excellis;
Fair be their wives, right lovesom, white and small;
Clere be thy virgyns, lusty under kellis:
London, thou art the Flour of Cities all.

Thy famous Maire, by pryncely governaunce,
With swerd of justice the ruleth prudently.
No Lord of Parys, Venyce, or Floraunce
In dignitie or honoure goeth to hynm nye.
He is exampler, loode-ster, and guye,
Principall patrone and roose orygynalle,
Above all Maires as maister moost worthy:
London, thou art the Flour of Cities all.

WILLIAM DUNBAR,
'IN HONOUR OF THE CITY OF LONDON'
(OR 'THE FLOUR OF CITIES ALL'),
CHOSEN BY LORD ARCHER

It is early morning
within this room:
without,
Dark and damp:
without and within,
stillness
Waiting for day:
not a sound but a
listening air.

LAURENCE BINYON,
'WINTER SUNRISE'

Borough Market

Produce at
Borough Market

Shakespeare's Globe Theatre

Things are a bit better now since William Blake
wrote this in the 1790s!

SIR TERENCE CONRAN

I wander thro' each charter'd street,
Near where the charter'd Thames does flow,
And mark in every face I meet
Marks of weakness, marks of woe.

In every cry of every Man,
In every Infant's cry of fear,
In every voice, in every ban,
The mind-forg'd manacles I hear.

How the Chimney-sweeper's cry
Every black'ning Church appalls;
And the hapless Soldier's sigh
Runs in blood down Palace walls.

But most thro' midnight streets I hear
How the youthful Harlot's curse
Blasts the new born Infant's tear,
And blights with plagues the marriage hearse.

WILLIAM BLAKE, 'LONDON'

The sun had long since in the lap
Of Thetis taken out his nap,
And, like a lobster boil'd, the morn
From black to red began to turn.

SAMUEL BUTLER,
FROM 'HUDIBRAS'

Looking East under
Millennium Bridge Northside

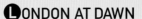

Up by 5 a-clock and, blessed by God, find all well, and by water to Paul's wharfe. Walked thence and saw all the town burned, and a miserable sight of Pauls church, with all the roofs fallen and the body of the Quire fallen into St Fayths – Paul's school also – Ludgate – Fleet Street – my father's house, and the church, and a good part of the Temple the like. So to Creeds lodging near the New Exchange, and there find him laid down upon a bed – the house all unfurnished, there being fears of the fire's coming to them.

SAMUEL PEPYS,
'THE GREAT FIRE – DIARY,
7TH SEPTEMBER 1666'

St Paul's from Ludgate Hill

By this time, like one who had set out on his way by night, and travelled through a region of smooth or idle dreams, our history now arrives on the confines, where daylight and truth meet us with a clear dawn, representing to our view, though at far distance, true colours and shapes.

JOHN MILTON
THE HISTORY OF ENGLAND

View from St Paul's

But when the sun in all his state Illumed the eastern skies, She passed through Glory's morning-gate, And walked in Paradise.

JAMES ALDRICH,
'A DEATH-BED'

View from Tate Modern

Listen to the Exhortation of the Dawn!
Look to this Day!
For it is Life, the very Life of Life.
In its brief course lie all the Verities and
Realities of your
Existence;
The Bliss of Growth,
The Glory of Action,
The Splendour of Beauty;
For Yesterday is but a Dream,
And Tomorrow is only a Vision:
But Today well lived makes Every Yesterday
a Dream of Happiness,
And every Tomorrow a Vision of Hope.
Look well therefore to this Day!
Such is the Salutation of the Dawn!

AUTHOR UNKNOWN,
SANSKRIT POEM

Millennium Bridge by Tate Modern

Oh, tenderly
the haughty day
Fills his blue urn
with fire.

RALPH WALDO EMERSON, 'ODE'

Tate Modern

Break the Skin, Quality Chop House, 94 Farringdon Road, *Progressive Working Class Caterer*; break the skin down the length of the sausage, split the pink, sizzling meat, gristle and fear. Gathering the strength for an assault on the book stalls. Comfortable within this old wood booth, hands around a mug of tea; mindless detachment. Gone back.

From the street there is nothing to be seen. No other use of this time.

Inside the booth, showing solidarity with the workers by eating their sausage sandwiches, you commissars of Stoke Newington, dipping the damp white bread in a gush of crimson vinegar. Squatting on a line of power, aligned, for once, with the drift of the city. Down with the water, from the ponds, the caves of Pentonville, rush with the Fleet, beside its ditch, swept with the dead dogs towards Thames. The domes of Old Bailey and St Paul's, the hulls of tenements, the office hulks. Everything in the end floats to Farringdon Road, deaths and libraries, sacks and tea-chests, confessions, testaments. The mysteries are shredded and priced. They are offered to the guided hand.

Fed, he plunges. In on a curve, the wall pulls, a knobbled blanket, galloping wave-pattern of the eye, buildings broken up, wide-horizon seizure, sweeping from Saffron Hill to Smithfield and St Bartholomew's Hospital, rail track gleams below, a dead ladder. Now there are eyes in the back of the head, in the neck, the skin is clairvoyant, hysterical sharpness of nerve: touch is sight. The rippling wall threatens the eye. Eye bleeds into holistic awareness.

All of the previous is there with him, he approaches himself, overtaking, rushing in, pain memories. The stalls are sheeted, roped. A lumpy bonehouse.

The MORNING STAR faces east: dim building titled to power. Red lettering, under the float of dust, making a sign but not a word. Low pulse red, receding. Where have you gone, Bill Sherman? Razor'd strips of cloud float in glass: postmortem windows.

The dealers huddle, converse in whispers. Slide a hand along the wall and penetrate the dome of Wren's machine, whale-melon vibrating in thought-star with other leviathans of the city, to swim back up Thames, the great churches, in a moment of Apocalypse, drowning human frenzy.

The rag-bundle punters connect themselves to the roped tables, secret gasses, pulped trees, socks, bones, melted pine veins; vortices of hope ignite. A Siberian railway platform. Clatter of wooden voices.

IAIN SINCLAIR, 'NO DAY SHOULD START
WITHOUT A SAUSAGE SANDWICH',
WHITE CHAPPELL SCARLET TRACINGS

The Smithfield Cafe

After university I got a job as a waitress in a restaurant on the Strand. I was immediately plunged into the night world of London. The catering trade proved to be a community of lost souls, finding family in the small hours between 3 and 7am. This was our time to play. Rich on tips and drunk on restaurant leftovers, I prowled the streets of the West End with my new best friends, the Lebanese busboys and the Antipodean waitresses. A Russian waiter fell in love with me. As dawn approached, he would walk me home through Smithfield meat market. Sometimes we would stop in at Ferrari's Cafe for a bacon sandwich, sitting among the big, burly, bloody, meat-packers who had just loaded their last side of pig in to the back of a lorry.

I was young and I felt like I could do what I liked. London loved me.

ZOE LEWIS

He who laughs not in the morning, laughs not at noon.

GREEK PROVERB

Eclipsed Lamppost on South Bank

Waterloo East

He used to skulk
in top hat and tattoos
slouching in a coat
that Wilde once wore

he had shoes
of bin liner
a fob watch of gold

he coughed
hand me down
cigarettes
drank Poormans sherry

i spoke to him
once
as the sky cracked

told me he was a tinker
that he had known love

she had been an acrobat
a tumbling star

'Finlays Circus of the Torrid'

a show
popular
with men
and midget hawks

but she vanished
on bareback
with horseshoe Shane
a man who could

make her stand
on her head
after hours

how time stabs

he died last week
this Dandy

on the street
hunched in a ball

his blankets of
tuesdays telegraph
blown away

delivering
unbearable news
of murder

in his breast pocket
they found a
sepia memory

a one-legged girl
flying through the air
with the greatest of unease
an uncomfortable smile
prepared
for a crash landing

his gold fob watch was still ticking

RALPH DARTFORD, 'DANDY'

I was born at 40 Grosvenor Road, near the Tate Gallery, where the Millbank Tower now stands and all my memories of London at dawn come from there or nearby.

On January 7th 1928 the banks of the Thames broke under the pressure of the water and our home was flooded, as were many other homes and offices, and though I was very tiny I remember seeing boats coming down the road to rescue people who were stranded there.

Twelve years later, in 1940, during the Blitz, we used to go out every night when the air raid sirens wailed and slept underground on the concrete basement floors at Thames House nearby. We emerged at dawn each day to see the damage done by the bombing.

One night a bomb landed in Westminster and five hundred people were killed, and across the river we could see the smoke rising over East London where the attacks on dockland inflicted even greater casualties.

And it was by the river at Wapping that many comrades and friends gathered to drop flowers in the river to commemorate Jack Dash the dockers' leader, poet and artist who loved the river and the people who worked on it.

Eleven years later, in 1951, as a young MP at the end of the post-war Labour government which had a tiny majority, we had many all-night sittings forced by the Tory opposition hoping to wear us out and often had breakfast at dawn on the terrace overlooking the river and watching London waking up and setting off for work.

I have lived in my present house for fifty years and both my dad and granddad were Londoners too, so all these memories, and many more, are firmly in my mind and many concern the river Thames with its busy traffic of tugs with their barges hooting as

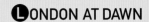

they moved up and down with their cargoes for the port of London.

London is a wonderful place to live, its population now enriched by people from all over the world but with a spirit that is unbeatable.

TONY BENN

Outside Waterloo Station

When feeling sad at home, I have often boarded a train or airport bus and gone to Heathrow where, from an observation gallery in Terminal 2 or from the top floor of the Renaissance Hotel along the north runway, I have drawn comfort from the sight of the ceaseless landing and take-off of aircraft.

From a car park beside O9L/27R, as the north runway is known to pilots, the 747 appears at first as a small brilliant white light, a star dropping towards earth. It has been in the air for 12 hours. It took off from Singapore at dawn. It flew over the Bay of Bengal, Delhi, the Afghan desert and the Caspian Sea. It traced a course over Romania, the Czech Republic, southern Germany and began its descent, so gently that few passengers would have noticed a change of tone in the engines, above the grey-brown, turbulent waters off the Dutch coast. It followed the Thames over London, turned north near Hammersmith (where the flaps began to unfold), pivoted over Uxbridge and straightened course over Slough. From the ground, the white light gradually takes shape as a vast two-storied body with four engines suspended like earrings beneath implausibly long wings. In the light rain, clouds of water form a veil behind the plane on its matronly progress towards the airfield. Beneath it are the suburbs of Slough. It is seven in the morning. In detached villas, kettles are being filled. A television is on in a living room with the sound switched off. Green and red shadows move silently across walls. The everyday. And above Slough is a plane that a few hours ago was flying over the Caspian Sea. Slough–the Caspian: the plane a symbol of worldliness, carrying within itself a trace of all the lands it has crossed; its eternal mobility offering an imaginative counterweight to feelings of stagnation and confinement.

Earlier on in its endless morning the plane was over the Malay Peninsula, a phrase in which there lingers the smells of guava and sandalwood. And now, a few metres above the earth which it has avoided for so long, the plane appears motionless, its nose raised upwards, seeming to pause before its sixteen rear wheels meet the tarmac with a blast of smoke that makes manifest its speed and weight.

On a parallel runway, an A340 ascends for New York and, over the Staines reservoir, retracts its flaps and wheels, which it won't require again until the descent over the white clapboard houses of Long Beach, 3,000 miles and eight hours of sea-and-cloud away. Visible through the heat haze of turbofans, other planes wait to start their journeys. All across the airfield, planes are on the move, their fins a confusion of colours against the grey horizon, like sails at a regatta.

Along the glass and steel back of Terminal 3 rest four giants, whose liveries indicate a varied provenance: Canada, Brazil, Pakistan, Korea. For a few hours, their wing-tips will lie only a few metres apart, before each set begins another journey into the stratospheric winds. As every ship turns into a gate, a choreographed dance begins. Trucks slip to the underbelly, black fuel hoses are fastened to the wings, a gangway bends its rectangular rubber lips over the fuselage. The doors of the holds are opened to withdraw battered aluminium cargo crates, perhaps containing fruit that only a few days ago hung from the branches of tropical trees or vegetables that had their roots in the soil of high silent valleys. Two men in overalls set up a small ladder next to one engine and open up its casing to reveal an intricate terrain of wires and small steel pipes. Sheets and pillows are lowered from

the front of one cabin. Passengers disembark for whom this ordinary English morning will have a supernatural tinge.

Nowhere is the appeal of the airport more concentrated than in the television screens which hang in rows from terminal ceilings, announcing the departure and arrival of flights, whose absence of aesthetic self-consciousness, whose workmanlike casing and pedestrian typefaces, do nothing to disguise their emotional charge nor imaginative appeal. Tokyo, Amsterdam, Istanbul. Warsaw, Seattle, Rio. The screens bear all the poetic resonance of the last line of James Joyce's Ulysses: at once a record of where the novel was written and no less importantly a symbol of the

cosmopolitan spirit behind its composition: 'Trieste, Zurich, Paris'. The constant calls of the screens, some accompanied by the impatient pulsing of a cursor, suggest with what ease our seemingly entrenched lives might be altered, were we to walk down a corridor and on to a craft that in a few hours would land us in a place of which we had no memories and where no one knew our name. How pleasant to hold in mind, through the crevasses of our moods, when lassitude and despair threaten, that there is always a plane taking off for somewhere, anywhere.

ALAIN DE BOTTON,
THE ART OF TRAVEL

I am lit

then I am spinning

as I turn to walk the last yards
to the tube
I know if I'd looked back
I would have seen
a condemned man's face
eaten by clocks

and how fast a night can pass

and how often love can't be

the light
the wheel
the glow of neon
are not enough to stop me
standing here exactly
my feet side by side
as if the curb's a cliff
and I've no fear of falling

ALISON DUNNE,
'I STAND EXACTLY HERE'

The surprise is that such an exultant poem about London, 'On Westminster Bridge', was written by a man celebrated above all and above all others for his Nature poetry. Those who are entangled in Wordsworth's Cumbrian roots might even feel a little left out. 'Not any thing to shew more fair'? Not Helvellyn, not Derwentwater, not Castle crags, not Aira Force, the Duddon Valley, or the mighty Scafell which formed the backdrop for one of the greatest portraits of Wordsworth. The Lake District has reason to feel a sense of injury!

Perhaps the occasion explains, even excuses it. Peace had broken out in the Anglo-French War and Wordsworth was on his way to see the French woman he had loved in his hot student years but had been unable to marry. She had had a child by him, a girl whom he had never seen.

The war had driven them apart. Now he was about to meet for what proved, it seems, an unusually happy few weeks. London then, as he set out for France, for old love's sake, was perhaps the beneficiary of this relief, this long awaited reunion, this crucial moment in his life.

That can be one explanation. Whatever the reason, the poem stands as one of the finest, most graphic poems ever written about the city by a man whose natural beat was without the city walls, though in truth he treats sleeping London itself as part of Nature.

MELVYN BRAGG

…Weeping may
endure for a night,
but joy cometh
in the morning.

FROM PSALM 30

Parliament

If anyone had ever told me that one of the advantages of being an MP was the all night sittings, I would never have believed them. The smell of stale sweat, beer and cigarettes invading your senses as you struggle to stay awake, fighting off the random aches in the head, shoulders and neck that invade your body when you keep it awake against its will are none of them attractive. The weary speeches and the numbing artificial light that fill the Chamber of the House of Commons only encourage the body to head for home and the comfort of bed. All this I had imagined, and all this was true. But I have to admit that there is one aspect to this experience which is quite magical.

To stay awake, when coffee's acrid flavour begins to make one feel sick, is to seek out fresh air. Clear the head, clear the lungs, startle the pasty flesh back to life. I staggered from the chamber and sought out the Terrace. That longed paved area which lies along the banks of the Thames. Where MPs crowd in the summer to drink and enjoy an escape from the forbidding corridors of the Palace, to feel the relaxation that water always gives.

As I approached the doors I could see the first faint shards of a new morning light. We had been sitting all night. I opened the door, and felt the cold spring air envelope me. I rubbed my face and eyes and moved to the wall overlooking the Thames. In the half-light it was grey, but I could detect the surging movement of the water in the shadows. I look up at St Thomas's Hospital to see the first strands of sunlight touch its upper towers and roofs.

I smelt a new day – not fresh, the London air is never fresh, but cleansed from the previous frantic day. There was noise from the traffic – it never ceases, but it was more muted, and more hopeful for a new day. I stood there and wallowed in the atmosphere as, slowly, the light picked out the picture before me more clearly. How long I stood there I don't know.

I was awakened by the division bell. Which burst in aggressively and discordantly on my dream. I walked back to the lobby, tired but revived.

MARJORIE MOWLAM

Sad soul,
take comfort,
nor forget
That sunrise
never failed
us yet.

CELIA THAXTER,
'THE SUNRISE NEVER
FAILED US YET'

Phoenix Restaurant in Brixton

Returning from a night shoot, on my last TV series one hot summer several years ago, I drove down the southern part of the Edgware Road just before dawn. All along its length, on both sides, the Arabic cafés were going full tilt, at the sidewalk tables men in long white robes smoked the tall nagileh pipes, women in hijabs strolled from shop to shop, chubby children in tow. Older teenagers in Western dress strolled in groups, or cruised up and down in BMWs and Jeeps. It was bizarre to witness London so totally transformed into a foreign city, with not a shred of its European roots showing.

It reminded me of how nocturnal and fun loving Arabs can be. When I was a young student, I shared a flat in Finchley with one of my best friends, who is a Palestinian. The place was always overrun with his politically active friends and I guess this is why the Special Branch decided to raid us. Now as you may or may not know, the standard tactic of the police is to bust your door down just before dawn, in the certain knowledge that you will be fast asleep and therefore disorientated and malleable. This they did to us with 20 armed officers and dogs, only to find that everybody in the house was wide awake; cooking food, running around tickling each other, messing about with hi-fi equipment and so on. The coppers were totally bewildered by this turn of events, and were so confused that they left quickly, with muttered apologies, and completely missed the multiple rocket launcher in the kitchen.

ALEXEI SAYLE, 'DAWN'

Brixton Market

Brixton Market

I love dis great polluted place
Where pop stars come to live their dreams
Here ravers come for drum and bass
And politicians plan their schemes,
The music of the world is here
Dis city can play any song
They came to here from everywhere
Tis they that made dis city strong.

A world of food displayed on streets
Where all the world can come and dine
On meals that end with bitter sweets
And cultures melt and intertwine,
Two hundred languages give voice
To fifteen thousand changing years
And all religions can rejoice
With exiled souls and pioneers.

I love dis overcrowded place
Where old buildings mark men and time
And new buildings all seem to race
Up to a cloudy dank skyline,
Too many cars mean dire air
Too many guns mean danger
Too many drugs mean be aware
Of strange gifts from a stranger.

It's so cool when the heat is on
And when it's cool it's so wicked
We just keep melting into one
Just like the tribes before us did,
I love dis concrete jungle still
With all its sirens and its speed
The people here united will
Create a kind of London breed.

BENJAMIN ZEPHANIAH, 'THE LONDON BREED'

I thought of London spread out in the sun, Its postal districts packed like squares of wheat.

PHILIP LARKIN

Alley in Soho

Dark house, by which once more I stand
Here in the long unlovely street,
Doors, where my heart was used to beat
So quickly, waiting for a hand,

A hand that can be clasp'd no more –
Behold me, for I cannot sleep,
And like a guilty thing I creep
At earliest morning to the door.

He is not here; but far away
The noise of life begins again,
And ghastly thro' the drizzling rain
On the bald streets breaks the blank day.

ALFRED, LORD TENNYSON,
'IN MEMORIAM: BEREAVEMENT IN
WIMPOLE STREET'

Alley in Covent Garden

Great Russell Street

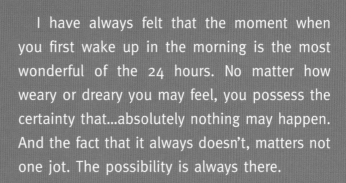

I have always felt that the moment when you first wake up in the morning is the most wonderful of the 24 hours. No matter how weary or dreary you may feel, you possess the certainty that...absolutely nothing may happen. And the fact that it always doesn't, matters not one jot. The possibility is always there.

MONICA BALDWIN
I LEAP OVER THE WALL

Workers on Battle Bridge Road

It was 5am when I crept out of my flat. London was just emerging out of a vermilion dawn and promising a fantastic, balmy day. I had finally decided to kill myself that very morning. Pity it wasn't pissing down.

And there was my old taxi; an almost defunct comrade, purchased from a totally defunct cabby, long since preceding me to the Great Goornicht. Nothingness!

The engine didn't start up immediately. 'Just my luck!' I cursed. But then it turned over and purred and I drove away from my family without looking back.

I knew where I was heading. A vast, solid Victorian wall, made out of dark grey bricks, just behind the main road where Kilburn High Road becomes Maida Vale; the back of a old sweatshop, possibly. I was going to drive right into it at 80 mph. It was as good a place as any to make my final exit. A perfect ending for a dramatist.

At first I drove with utmost care. Police cars often lurked in side roads in the very early morning.

And there was the wall of dirty bricks straight ahead. I pushed my foot down and the wall hurtled towards me.

But almost at once I knew I wasn't going to be allowed to get away with it. That man

Ironworks, Battle Bridge Road

in the taxi mirror was watching me with a beady eye. 'Don't be ridiculous! Turn round. Go home!' I kept my foot on the pedal, trying not to hear.

My voice got louder. 'Ask yourself. Who are you really trying to hurt here?'

'Only me!'

'Listen! The arrogance of the man,' he said, his eyebrows raised very high in the mirror. 'Why don't you just let the shit pour out of your ears for just a minute?'

'Bastard,' I answered as I slammed on the brakes. The taxi screeched to a stop.

I was no more than a few feet away from the wall and I was definitely not dead. And I knew I just was lumbered with getting on with the rest of my life. I closed my eyes and could hear the birds singing the beginning of the day I wasn't supposed to be in.

I turned the cab around and drove to Vallance Road in Whitechapel, to buy some piping-hot bagels for the family at the All Night Bagel Shop.

The bagels were just coming out of the oven, the steam of life rising from them. The night cabbies were yucknering at the counter, each demanding to be served first so that they could get off home to Ilford and Hendon to their steaming-hot, sleeping wives; now one quarter awake and ready to be stirred with a nice little bit of conjugaling.

I was also on my way home, with a bag of hot bagels for the family.

I drove my taxi most of the way, but parked the old girl somewhere near the Catholic church in Quex Road and walked the rest. I felt a sudden rush of euphoria and exhilaration as I walked into the wind. All this was extra. I had finally got rid of the crazy guy on my shoulder. The early morning sky was liquid gold! 'Lochaim!' To life! I gulped it down and hurried home.

When I turned the key and opened the door Erica was standing there, waiting, her face long and drawn.

'I've bought some hot bagels for breakfast,' I said, and kissing her, 'Incidentally, I'm never taking drugs again.' She smiled knowingly, somewhere between hope and suspicion.

And I never did use from that day forth. For the last 27 years aspirin has been my outer limit.

And later that morning, after taking the kids to school, Erica and I returned to the back streets behind Kilburn to look for our taxi. I thought I knew where I had left her but, as had happened so often before, I turned out to be mistaken. The old girl had vanished. We searched for more than an hour but got nowhere.

'Maybe tomorrow you'll remember,' Erica said as we made our way home.

For the rest of that week when the kids were in school we combed the streets between Kilburn and Maida Vale but we never did find it. Some other madman must have found her and was now flying her crazily through the sky.

It seemed appropriate somehow that I should lose her on the very day that I re-discovered my sanity.

These days whenever I do feel a little mad and start to act outrageously, which is quite often, my son-in-law Mark smiles and remarks, 'Where's your old taxi, Bernard? Shall we go and look for it?'

BERNARD KOPS, FROM *SHALOM BOMB:
SCENES FROM MY LIFE*

'My dear wife Carrie and I have just been a week in our new house, 'The Laurels', Brickfield Terrace, Holloway – a nice six-roomed residence, not counting basement, with a front breakfast-parlour. We have a little front garden; and there is a flight of ten steps up to the front door, which, by-the-by, we keep locked with the chain up. Cummings, Gowing and our other intimate friends always come to the little side entrance, which saves the servant the trouble of going up to the front door, thereby taking her from her work. We have a nice back garden which runs down to the railway. We were rather afraid of the noise of the trains at first, but the landlord said we should not notice them after a bit and took £2 off the rent. He was certainly right; and beyond the cracking of the garden wall at the bottom, we have suffered no inconvenience.'

CHARLES POOTER
IN *THE DIARY OF A NOBODY*
BY GEORGE AND WEEDON GROSSMITH

St Pancras Station

Inside St Pancras Station

I used to wake up next to Boadicea. They say she's buried under Platform 9. I looked right into the station from my lovely room in Culross Buildings behind King's Cross. And from the roof garden, I thought I could feel the whole of Britain rising in an instant. The trains were going north; the Telecom Tower buzzed into life. And yet on that roof, on a winter morning, with the 5.21 to Peterborough sliding out of the station, it was mostly the past that seemed to speak. I really love that place. It's a corner of London still mad with Victorian grandeur. For years now it has lived with the threat of demolition. But it doesn't want to go. People believe it will last forever. You see the remnants of a place called Agar Town from up there. It disappeared to make way for the great railway terminals. From the roof of Culross Buildings you can see the world as it used to be; the gasometers built in the 1860s, the Regent's Canal, the arch of St Pancras, the Great Northern Hotel. And down below there are the cobbled streets. The German Gymnasium stands like some beautiful monument to the enthusiasms of the dead. I will always love this secretive London. Britain's industrial past is nowhere more present than this. I still hear the sound of the trains as I sleep.

ANDREW O'HAGAN, 'A LONDON VIEW'

Trafalgar Square

I know London very well: my history is spread out over the city just as Dickens's was. So many of the crucial moments of my life have taken place in this place or that: my childhood in south London, my school in Chelsea, my first job in South Kensington, my first job in the theatre in Waterloo, my drama school in Chalk Farm, my virginity lost in Belsize Park (phew), this relationship in Earls Court, that affair in Notting Hill Gate – as I walk round the city I feel like a drowning man, my past rushing past, blocking out the present, ghosts beckoning sometimes seductively, sometimes mockingly. I could write with tender affection about so many parts of the city – including the City, indeed, where I worked for a year – but if I'm asked point blank, as I was, to write about the part of London that matters most to me, I have, mumbling and blushing, to admit that it is the West End. It's so boring; so predictable. I mean, what a luvvie! But it's no good. If you woke me up at four in the morning and said: 'Where in London do you feel you really belong?' then I would without hesitation say, St Martin's Lane. There is a particular view, as you come down from Upper St Martin's Lane, just at the top of the lane itself, from which you can see the London Coliseum with its gaudy revolving glass ball, and you can just glimpse St Martin-in-the-Fields, and sense by implication Trafalgar Square and Whitehall and Parliament beyond, which has never failed to stop my heart.

I have worked frequently in both the theatres in St Martin's Lane, the Duke of York's and the Albery, and even when the shows have been disasters, working there on a daily basis is still a peculiar kind of a thrill. It's something to do with the shops and restaurants in the two cross streets with Charing Cross Road – Cecil Court with its esoteric and specialist bookshops, St Martin's Place, with

Sheekey's restaurant – something to do with memories of meals eaten, and plays and operas and films (from when the Coliseum was a Cinerama House) seen, but more to do with the romance of London. Its breadth and grandeur, and my dreams of Up West as a kid from Streatham to whom this pivotal point was the heart of the metropolis, where everything seemed to matter, and to be touched by history. It is full of theatres, to be sure, but more importantly, it is theatre, and everything that passes through it seems to acquire a heightened power.

SIMON CALLOW, 'WEST END WILLIE'

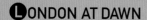

'Oh what a glorious morning is this.'

SAMUEL ADAMS

Early risers on Nelson Column

There is, of late, an extraordinary new vitality to London. The city is radiant and self-aware, and it no longer feels like a venerated museum which the whole world feels obliged to visit because it is so cutely Olde Worlde. Even grumpy Londoners like myself who have to grapple with these pilgrims do now concede that there is something exhilarating in the air. This is qualitatively different from the eighties when shallow yuppies seemed dangerously close to taking over the metropolis. In her diary entry on the 26 May, 1926, Virginia Woolf wrote: 'London is enchanting. I step out upon a tawny-coloured magic carpet and get carried into beauty.' Today she would look down on a place less beautiful perhaps; infinitely more unsettling, at times like Babel, yet magnetically attractive and engaging.

London beguiles because it is so un-English. From being an endless problem for the capital, diversity has become potent, drawing loungers of an altogether different sort. Long before the post-war migration from the colonies, Arthur Conan Doyle's Sherlock Holmes believed London had become a 'great cesspool into which all the loungers of the Empire are irresistibly drained'.

The last profound shake-up in London was in the sixties when the city became a shrine to youth, sex and freedom. London was pretending that we, black and Asian Britons, had never arrived. We lurked at the fringes, hidden, trying not to draw unwanted attention. Now Britons in love with diversity have claimed the capital. There is at present no other Western city which can match this.

This emerging London is sharp and cosmopolitan. It is where many of the young love Fun-Da-Mental, a group of multiracial musicians led by the devout Muslim Aki Navaz, who merges rap with Sufi and black music. Or Asian Dub Foundation with young

British Bangladeshis mixing hard lyrics with yielding, soft harmonies. Both these pop groups are aggressively demanding of their right to this city. Their songs are raw and real; they rile against racism, exclusion and all inherited categories, and celebrate instead the essential hybridity of their own lives. You could fill a book with examples of these artists who are remaking London.

The hugely talented actress Neena Wadia feels embraced by this revolution: 'How London has changed since I first came over 12 years ago. It feels like everyone has a stake in this city. You can be yourself and find an outlet for your talents, your stories.' Every group of newcomers into London disturbs the meaning of belonging and home. Immigration changes those who move and the places they move to. Neither can ever be the same, especially not a promiscuous city like London which is ever more hungry for contact and less afraid of contamination.

YASMIN ALIBHAI-BROWN,
'THE COLOUR OF LONDON'

So sinks the day-star in the ocean bed, And yet anon repairs his drooping head, And tricks his beams, and with new-spangled ore Flames in the forehead of the morning sky.

JOHN MILTON, *LYCIDIAS*

Sweet Phosphor, bring the day
Whose conquering ray
May chase these fogs;
Sweet Phosphor, bring the day!

Sweet Phosphor, bring the day!
Light will repay
The wrongs of night;
Sweet Phosphor, bring the day!

FRANCIS QUARLES, 'EMBLEMS'

Looking into Leicester Square

Vendor at Covent
Garden Flower Market

Covent-garden Market, when it was market morning, was wonderful company. The great waggons of cabbages, with growers' men and boys lying asleep under them, and with sharp dogs from market-garden neighbourhoods looking after the whole, were as good as a party. But one of the worst night sights I know in London, is to be found in the children who prowl about this place; who sleep in the baskets, fight for the offal, dart at any object they think they can lay their thieving hands on, dive under the carts and barrows, dodge the constables, and are perpetually making a blunt pattering on the pavement of the Piazza with the rain of their naked feet. A painful and unnatural result comes of the comparison one is forced to institute between the growth of corruption as displayed in the so much improved and cared for fruits of the earth, and the growth of corruption as displayed in these all uncared for (except inasmuch as ever-hunted) savages.

There was early coffee to be got about Covent-garden Market, and that was more company – warm company, too, which was better. Toast of a very substantial quality, was likewise procurable: though the towzled-headed man who made it, in an inner chamber within the coffee-room, hadn't got his coat on yet, and was so heavy with sleep that in every interval of toast and coffee he went off anew behind the partition into complicated crossroads of choke and snore, and lost his way directly.

CHARLES DICKENS,
THE UNCOMMERCIAL TRAVELLER (1861)

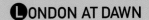

In my early years as an MP I often saw the dawn before I got home. All is now different in these politically correct days of breast-feeding and family-friendly hours. Now, as soon as MPs are elected to Parliament, they whinge about having to attend it. I spent many a sultry summer's night in a suffocating House of Commons committee room watching the Opposition exploit its sole power against a government with a huge majority – filibuster and delay.

The silver lining to the cloud of sleepless nights and baggy eyes was to limp down to the Terrace as the sun came up over distant St Paul's. In front stood Westminster Bridge, on whose predecessor Wordsworth began his lyrical sonnet about the city at dawn:

Ne'er saw I, never felt a calm so deep!
The river glideth at his own sweet will:
Dear God! The very houses seem asleep;
And all that mighty heart is lying still.

Whilst London's traffic was never entirely stilled, on those occasions I felt the peace and unity with nature which contrasted so dramatically with the all-too-human conflicts of party politics.

NEIL HAMILTON

Waterloo Place

Having left the square, Dickens now saw the odd stragglers trying to hold their own in the wintry blast. It was the early hours of Christmas morning and a few people still had a mind to cut through the snow to distant hearths. Dickens watched these bravers of the elements with their thick cloak-coats flapping in the unceasing wind. He passed through the snow-filled courtyards of Lincoln's Inn that, during the day, were thronged with bum-bailiffs, clerks, solicitors and legal magicians who could turn black into its opposite in the interest of justice and who knew the top and bottom of a codicil as well as Dickens knew the backbone of an Aberdeen kipper. Banks of snow had by now made many of the passages and courts impassable. Not much chance of the kings of rodentry around here, might have been Dickens' thought as he negotiated the rather difficult geography brought on by the weather.

Even on his most blighted of nights at this most blighted of hours, Dickens encountered little knots of troubled people who huddled in the closes and passages, beyond the enquiring lamps of the peelers. Wispy people, with no more blood in their veins than a cockroach, did their huddling in cold stairways and doorways, and, as Dickens passed, he would often pause and look into the dark recesses. No shadow could hide them from his sharp eye, and though they did not like the eye of anyone to fall upon them, Dickens' two green ones caused them no consternation.

When he arrived at Dumpling Passage, Dickens took up his position on the wall at the end of the passage, which allowed him a good view. Sitting, he looked down at the snow-strewn alley and looked up at the little houses. Few lights could be seen. Little noise could be heard. Even Dumpling Passage seemed to have been subdued by inclemency.

A JOHN BIRD,
FROM *DICKENS THE SOCIALLY MOBILE CAT*

Regent Street

Piccadilly Circus

Damp
Dank
Sweaty Streets
Clever Bastards
Never meet
Hours on Trains
Living high
Underground.
Soho
Noho
Hobo
Nothing Sound
Now
Here
Nowhere
London
Found.

GORDON RODDICK,
'LONDON ROUND'

It is very strange out West, down Piccadilly, on Saturday morning. There are women such as I have never seen before, beautiful, flowing women, with a pride and grace you never meet in the provinces. The proud ruling air of these women of the stately West is astounding; I stand still and stare at them.

D.H. LAWRENCE,
'LETTER TO MAY CHAMBERS,
HOLBROOK, FEBRUARY 1909'

Regent Street from Piccadilly Circus

Firstly, I'd just like to say how honoured I feel to be speaking on this sad day. For those of you who didn't see Chet in his final years, I hope I can bring some peace into your lives, and offer you the comfort of knowing that he died doing something important.

The first time I saw Chet, I was sitting in a café on Oxford Street and he walked past. Simple as that. I'll be blunt and say he looked no different to the scores of beggars we see every day on London's streets. And yet, and I'm not just saying this, there was something else to him. I couldn't put my finger on it at the time, but it grabbed my attention as sure as a slap in the face. I can remember watching him shuffling up the street in his dirty rags, his worn-out shoes, bringing one hand up to his mouth every now and then to take a drag on a cigarette butt someone had tossed in the gutter. He was one of those people you didn't want to look at, because you're ashamed of what you have and scared that they'll take it from you.

I know I'm not painting a very flattering picture, and I know they say you shouldn't speak ill of the dead. But I also know that Chet valued truth and order more than anything, and he'd have wanted me to tell it like it was.

Have you ever noticed that if someone starts talking about BMWs, you start seeing more of them on the roads? Well, that's how it was with me and Chet. I had my lunch at that same café for five years and I'd never noticed him before – and I'm a journalist, so I pride myself on being observant. Yet after that day, I couldn't help but notice him, shuffling down that pavement. I began to wonder how I could've missed him. I noticed small changes. Mangy off-white trainers replaced what were once smart leather business shoes. Cuts, bruises and cold sores passed across his face, fading and returning, mirroring the seasons. Chet aroused my journalist's curiosity. Where did he come from? Why was he here? Why wasn't anyone taking care of him?

I know there are many of you out there today who still wonder the same things. Why didn't he ask for help? Why didn't he come home? And others who knew him while he was still MD of Dotcom.com, and still can't believe that the smartly dressed executive they addressed memos to, is the same man I knew. The same man I wrote my feature about. The same man who was so brutally cut down in the midst of his battle against chaos.

For those who haven't seen Chet since his school days, I'll backtrack a bit. Chet didn't have a harsh home life. He was lucky enough to go to university. He rode the Internet boom and became one of Soho's most sought-after web designers. That's right – the same man. The same man you saw in the newspaper photographs, with his ratty clothes and dirty face. As we know, the Internet bubble burst, just like that. Chet's company went bankrupt and his colleagues, some of whom are out there today, went home. But Chet didn't. The last his wife Sam and daughter Carly saw of him was when he left for work a little over 18 months ago.

Chet walked out of his office on Poland Street and walked up to Oxford Street, turning right to head for Tottenham Court Road station. He was in a daze, trying to work things out. It's a big thing, riding a wave and then getting dumped. You come up spluttering for breath, finding it hard to know which way is up. And that's what Chet was doing that afternoon, walking along Oxford Street, when he noticed something. Something that changed his life and also, in a roundabout way, shortened it considerably. No one was walking in a straight line. Everyone was ducking and diving, weaving and

St. James's Park

wending, bumping into people, skipping around people. It was chaos. And Chet decided, right then, that if he could control that chaos, a few other things might fall into place.

That might sound crazy to you, but, when you think about it, it's amazingly clear reasoning from someone who has just had his world collapse around him. And think about this. If each of us took some responsibility for the chaos that is blossoming around us – the graffiti, the unloved kids with hate in their hearts, the pollution, just the general uncaring attitude we've adopted by proxy – wouldn't this world be a much nicer place?

So that was when Chet decided to go straight. He started walking a straight line, along Oxford Street. When he got to the junction of Tottenham Court Road, he thought about it and turned around – there was only so much one person could do. That became his life's work. From Tottenham Court Road down to Bond Street, mainly during the lunchtime and evening rush hours, Chet was trying to impose some rationality on the world.

This went on for 18 months. Chet never left the street. He walked up and down, sleeping in doorways, scavenging in bins for food. It's amazing what we leave behind. There's a whole class of people out there, surviving on what we throw away. Makes you think. Sam called the police, like any dutiful wife would, and the police did their job as best they could, but they couldn't reconcile the dishevelled man on the street with the successful web designer. And even if they had, it wouldn't have made a difference.

When I wrote my story, Chet had been out on the street for more than a year. He was perfectly coherent when I spoke to him. He'd had a few teeth knocked out in a fight but he knew what he was doing, and he wasn't ready to go home. His feet were covered in blisters, but he was used to it, and he wasn't going to give up when he felt he was finally making some progress. Up and down, up and down. He didn't even want to stop for the interview. It was only by offering a meal at the café that I got him to take a break. And even then he couldn't stop looking through the window, judging the sea of people, pointing out how they were walking much more straighter than this time ten months ago.

In my mind, Chet was a rational human being, trying to operate in an irrational world. Which was why I agreed to withhold his name, and use silhouetted photographs. All I can say now is how sorry I am I didn't give Sam and Carly one last chance to see Chet – the chance my story could have provided – but I'm glad Sam asked me to speak today. I'm honoured, and I thank her for her forgiveness. I don't think this is the time or the place to go into the gruesome particulars of Chet's run-in with the white van man – I'm sure you all read about it in the papers – but I'd like to assure you that Chet died doing something that he believed in. And how many of us, if we died right now, could say the same thing?

Thank you.

MILES FOTHERINGTON,
'STRAIGHT – A EULOGY BY GARY KEMBLE'

St James's Park/Fence

Behold how
brightly breaks
the morning!
Though
bleak our lot,
our hearts
are warm.

JAMES KENNEY,
*'BEHOLD HOW
BRIGHTLY BREAKS'*

Man with Ducks in St James's Park

183

Awake,
my glory;
awake, lute
and harp:
I myself
will awake
right early.

PSALM 57

Oxford Street

It's hard to know how to connect it –
The launderette, the toilet down the passage,
The stale, brittle leaves
That rustle beside empty park benches
And shred
And get in my eyes,
And old ladies, stiff and silent and unseeing
In their obscure worlds
Except for an occasional, hesitant smile,
And you.
You, waving from a high window,
You, squirrelish, eating chestnuts,
Or in your pink suit
Like an ice-cream your friend said
When seen walking down Oxford Street,
Like a strawberry Cornetto – your favourite.

And you being lower class
And you living with your mother
In one room,
Because your father was a drunk
Who died young
And kept a diary
Which you kept and read
And wondered about
Because he gave your mother her glass eye
And you your bony wrists
Which were broken when he swung you around –
Daddy! Daddy!
And you bunking off school
To eat jam roll in the Ossington Coffee Tavern
(Which is no longer there now),
And you dancing,

And your scandalous 'Play it again!'
In the Thirties,
And you walking down Marylebone High Street.

So how shall I place you?
A loner, like me,
A queen to me,
Beside Buckingham Palace
And those ornate empty rituals
With cannons and carriages,
And those merging points of light
Off the towers
By the Thames,
And those flowerless winter beds in Marylebone
And that hardware shop
Which is still there, I think?
I'll look at a sky that's pink and orange and white
A sky like dessert
Or ice cream
A sky fit for eating,
Like a strawberrry Cornetto – your favourite.
And scoop out a woundful.

IAN McLACHLAN, 'HELLO DOLLY!'

Clothing the palpable and familiar With golden exhalations of the dawn.

SAMUEL TAYLOR COLERIDGE,
FROM *THE DEATH OF WALLENSTEIN*

Phonebox on Grosvenor Road

I suggested a doubt, that if I were to reside in London, the exquisite zest with which I relished it in occasional visits might go off, and I might grow tired of it.

JOHNSON. 'Why, Sir, you find no man, at all intellectual, who is willing to leave London. No, Sir, when a man is tired of London, he is tired of life; for there is in London all that life can afford'.

JAMES BOSWELL, *LIFE OF JOHNSON*

Regent Street at Christmas Time

LONDON AT DAWN

Yet there was round thee such a dawn
Of light, ne'er seen before,
As fancy never could have drawn,
And never can restore.

CHARLES WOLFE,
'TO MARY'

Looking East on Grosvenor Road

We bring roses, beautiful fresh roses, Dewy as the morning and coloured like the dawn.

THOMAS BUCHANAN READ
THE NEW PASTORAL BOOK

Battersea Power Station

Golden slumbers
kiss your eyes
Smiles awake you
when you rise.

THOMAS DEKKER

Archway

When all men were all asleep the snow came flying,
In large white flakes falling on the city brown,
Stealthily and perpetually settling and loosely lying,
Hushing the latest traffic of the drowsy town;
Deadening, muffling, stifling its murmurs failing;
Lazily and incessantly floating down and down:
Silently sifting and veiling road, roof and railing;
Hiding difference, making unevenness even,
Into angles and crevices softly drifting and sailing.
All night it fell, and when full inches seven
It lay in the depth of its uncompacted lightness,
The clouds blew off from a high and frosty heaven;
And all work earlier for the unaccustomed brightness
Of the winter dawning, the strange unheavenly glare:
The eye marvelled – marvelled at the dazzling whiteness;
The ear hearkened to the stillness of the solemn air;
No sound of wheel rumbling nor of foot falling,
And the busy morning cries came thin and spare.
Then boys I heard, as they went to school, calling,
They gathered up the crystal manna to freeze
Their tongues with tasting, their hands with snowballing;
Or rioted in a drift, plunging up to the knees;
Or peering up from under the white-mossed wonder,
'O look at the trees!' they cried, 'O look at the trees!'
With lessened load a few carts creak and blunder,
Following along the white deserted way,
A country company long dispersed asunder:
When now already the sun, in pale display
Standing by Paul's high dome, spread forth below
His sparkling beams, and awoke the stir of the day.
For now doors open, and war is waged with the snow;
And trains of sombre men, past tale of number,
Tread long brown paths, as toward their toil they go:

But even for them awhile no cares encumber
Their minds diverted; the daily word is unspoken,
The daily thoughts of labour and sorrow slumber
At the sight of the beauty that greets them, for the charm they
have broken.

ROBERT BRIDGES, 'LONDON SNOW'

Sunrise on Bench, Waterlow Park

Waterlow Park

The wind that sighs before the dawn Chases the gloom of night, The curtains of the East are drawn, And suddenly – 't is light.

SIR LEWIS MORRIS,
'LE VENT DE L'ESPRIT'

Waterlow Park

Every day should be passed as if it were to be our last.

PUBLIUS SYRUS

Highgate Cemetery

The childhood
shows the man,
As morning shows
the day.

JOHN MILTON,
FROM *PARADISE REGAINED*

Men in Trees on Primrose Hill

If I had to choose a religion, the sun, as the universal giver of life, would be my god.

NAPOLEON BONAPARTE

Dewdrops on Primrose Hill

Light on Primrose Hill

Time writes no wrinkle on thine azure brow, Such as creation's dawn beheld, thou rollest now.

LORD BYRON,
FROM *CHILDE HAROLD'S PILGRIMAGE*

Time to go Home

And the day star arise in your hearts.

NEW TESTAMENT

LONDON AT DAWN

Houses, churches, mixed together,
Streets unpleasant in all weather;
Prisons, palaces contiguous,
Gates, a bridge, the Thames irriguous.

Gaudy things enough to tempt ye,
Showy outsides, insides empty;
Bubbles, trades, mechanic arts,
Coaches, wheelbarrows and carts.

Warrants, bailiffs, bills unpaid,
Lords of laundresses afraid;
Rogues that nightly rob and shoot men,
Hangmen, aldermen and footmen.

Lawyers, poets, priests, physicians,
Noble, simple, all conditions:
Worth beneath a threadbare cover,
Villainy bedaubed all over.

Women black, red, fair and grey,
Prudes and such as never pray,
Handsome, ugly, noisy, still,
Some that will not, some that will.

Many a beau without a shilling,
Many a widow not unwilling;
Many a bargain, if you strike it:
This is London! How d'ye like it?

JOHN BANCKS,
'A DESCRIPTION OF LONDON'

Chelsea Power Station

Hampstead Heath

Sweet day,
so cool,
so calm,
so bright,
The bridal of
the earth
and sky.

GEORGE HERBERT,
'VIRTUE'

Early morning. Regent's Park. I have gone for a walk (it used to be a run), and the community of walkers slows the pace for a bit of a chat. I started it to keep fit, but these days it's as much for the social side. The regulars – rough sleepers and City workers; the gardeners who labour so hard all year round, including in sheeting rain; the few (illegal) cyclists; the animals in the zoo, who always seem to be chatting to us but are probably just commenting on the weather – as we do.

As the dawn gets into its stride, you can see people's faces change. The dogs and their owners look less alike. Those flashing dog collars that show in the dark look almost modest in design. And people begin to smile. London is always thought of as unfriendly. If you get on the tube, it tends to be silent. But London's buses are chatty, and Regent's Park is even chattier. Everyone says hello. If you miss a few days, you are asked if you were ill. If you are early or late there's a solicitous: 'Is everything all right?'

I love my morning walk, and I love the people I see most days. I don't know their names. But I notice when they are not there – and they notice me as well. That's the best of London – and it's extraordinarily beautiful as well. Regent's Park at dawn is secret, buds opening, flowers just releasing their scent, mist over the grass. And the walk at dawn – just as it has opened – makes one notice the slightest change of temperature and season – and be glad to be alive.

RABBI JULIA NEUBERGER, CHIEF EXECUTIVE,
KING'S FUND, 'EARLY MORNING LONDON'

Couple on Hampstead Heath

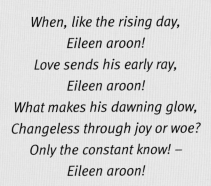

When, like the rising day,
Eileen aroon!
Love sends his early ray,
Eileen aroon!
What makes his dawning glow,
Changeless through joy or woe?
Only the constant know! –
Eileen aroon!

'EILEEN AROON'
GERALD GRIFFIN

The Royal Albert Hall

221

My morning office provides the most magnificent view of the world's greatest city. Executives may boast of their lavish suites on the 30th floor of paper-pushing empires, and even the London Eye, surely London's answer to the elegance of the Eiffel Tower, with its 400-foot high vistas, pales by comparison.

For my morning office, although ear-splittingly noisy, far from luxurious, and often quite violent, offers me an unparalleled view of London from a height of 1500 feet. It is the Capital Radio Flying Eye, a twin-engined GA-7 Cougar light aircraft. From the right-hand seat, I have flown more than 1,100,000 miles over the traffic-choked streets of our capital city, broadcasting to the millions of listeners to our breakfast show.

And the sight of this wonderful, vibrant, infuriating, concreted, verdant giant coming to life each morning never fails to utterly impress and bring a sense of wonderment. The juxtaposition of our architectural heritage, imbued with so much history it makes Americans faint, with the new, stark arrogance of, say, Canary Wharf, makes London a never-ending flight of discovery. But dawn is when the city really goes to town.

As the sun rises, it bathes each building in a dusky, pink glow. In this quite beautiful, enchanting light, London casts a spell so powerful that we forget we can't park, that the price of everything is insane and our public transport system is run by the Marquis de Sade. Magically, every irritant of our love/hate relationship fades in the early light. Look how the Thames runs pink, like a pulsating artery, how the dome of St Paul's remains architecturally awe-inspiring, how the glass of our skyscrapers reflects the optimism of their inhabitants. See how the dew is still on the surprisingly vast parklands, how only the pigeons see the true, empty elegance of

Trafalgar Square, and how the bridges across the Thames each contain their very own Lowry figures.

Above all, this dawn love affair has that irreplaceable ingredient for romantic excitement – it's a secret. At dawn, it feels as though it's just you and the city. London awaits your pleasure, to be explored at your will, to revel in and marvel at. Just the two of you.

Thirty minutes later, 10 million other lovers invade what was, just for a tantalising moment, yours alone. And that brief moment is good enough for me – and has me yearning for the next time this beautiful city decides to share that magnificent, achingly tender, dawn magic.

RUSS KANE

But with the morning cool reflection came.

SIR WALTER SCOTT,
CHRONICLES OF THE CANONGATE

Little Venice

And God called
the light Day
and the darkness
he called Night
And the evening
and the morning
were the first day.

GENESIS 1:5

Little Venice

Full many a glorious morning have I seen.

WILLIAM SHAKESPEARE,
'SONNET XXXIII'

Thames at Richmond with boats

I decided to
go to London,
for the purpose
of hearing the
Strand roar,
which I think
one does want,
after a day or two
in Richmond.

VIRGINIA WOOLF
DIARY

Under Bridge in Richmond with Boats

In London the masses can be seen on a scale and in conditions not to be seen anywhere else in the world.

I have been told, for example, that on Saturday nights, half a million working men and women and their children spread like the ocean all over town, clustering particularly in certain districts, and celebrate their Sabbath all night long until five o'clock in the morning, in other words guzzle and drink like beasts to make up for a whole week.

FROM *WINTER NOTES ON SUMMER IMPRESSIONS*
BY FYODOR DOSTOYEVSKY

Seen from the air this ominous August dawn, the Thames is a diamond-dusted silver ribbon. The aeroplanes follow the river faithfully, nose to tail, as they descend over south-west London, giving panoramic views of the individual boathouses, Putney Bridge, the green spaces of the Hurlingham Club and Fulham Palace gardens, straining and whining as they throttle back over the salubrious complacence of Barnes, then whistling on through the malty cumulus clouds issuing from the chimneys of Mortlake's brewery. On they roar, hooting and wrangling across the 400 botanic acres at Kew, from there to shade Richmond's millennial prosperity with their wings; then on, down lower still, to the shattered concentration of Hounslow, its double-glazed schools and uproarious bedrooms, where those on the ground can if they so desire look up and check the colour of the pilot's tie.

HELEN SIMPSON, FROM 'MILLENNIUM BLUES',
HEY YEAH RIGHT GET A LIFE

Thames
in Richmond 235

Anthony and I had been friends for a couple of years, and whenever we met up, usually over a couple of beers, the conversation would inevitably turn to how the early morning photos were coming along. I'd always be really enthusiastic and suggest locations and buildings that might be worth checking out. This enthusiasm was to be my downfall, for as soon as the project had some backing Anthony asked if I would be prepared to ferry him around!

Outward journeys would be almost silent until we had a sense of dawn's approach, when Anthony would start getting very excited about the quality of light. I'd pick up on his mood and start telling him what I knew about the history of the area. By the break of dawn we'd both be pretty fired up and thoroughly awake. One morning I suggested trying Blackheath, as the panorama there facing east has hardly changed in 200 years. Anthony was immediately drawn to the tea-hut and was really pleased with the shots of that and the cheerful ladies who run it. As dawn hadn't quite risen, I said, 'Let's try the Thames Barrier next.' Ten minutes later we'd climbed a couple of fences and were out on a concrete jetty watching the sun rise over the barrier, with a cup of tea and an egg and sausage sandwich. Anthony will always remember that dawn for its light – I'll remember clambering over fences and feeling like a kid again and, of course, that sandwich.

NICK MORTIMER, THE BLACK CAB DRIVER WHO DROVE
THE AUTHOR AROUND IN THE EARLY MORNINGS

Nick Mortimer

CREDITS

Grateful acknowledgement is made to the following for permission to reproduce extracts used in this book:

Penguin Books Ltd for permission to use material from:
The Art of Travel by Alain de Botton
(page 117)

David Higham Associates for permission to use material from:
The Medusa Frequency by Russell Hoban
(page 115)

Granta Publishing for permission to use material from:
White Chappell Scarlet Tracings by Iain Sinclair
(page 103)

Faber and Faber Publishing for permission to use material from:
'The Whitsun Weddings' by Philip Larkin
(page 134)

Peters Fraser & Dunlop for permission to use material from:
Hey Yeah Right Get a Life by Helen Simpson
(page 233)

John Murray Publishing for permission to use material from:
'Devonshire Street W1, 1954' by John Betjeman

The Copyright in Anthony Sher's words is retained by the author.